D1453880

The John Hancock Center

The John Hancock Center

Photographs by Ezra Stoller

Introduction by Yasmin Sabina Khan

building blocks

Princeton Architectural Press • New York

The BUILDING BLOCKS series presents the masterworks of modern architecture through the iconic images of acclaimed architectural photographer Ezra Stoller.

Contents

Introduction

Yasmin Sabina Khan

AN IMPASSIONED DESIRE for dignity of character and unambiguous structural articulation has inspired Chicago's architects for more than a century. It was in Chicago that Louis Sullivan wrote "form ever follows function"; Ludwig Mies van der Rohe's dictum "less is more" succinctly articulates the architectural ethos of the city. Although enthusiasm for the principles of visual simplicity and frank structural expression has inevitably waxed and waned over the years, in the early 1960s these precepts were in favor and imbued Chicago's architecture with a practical direction. The John Hancock Center, a one hundred-story mixed-use skyscraper designed collaboratively by architect Bruce J. Graham and structural engineer Fazlur R. Khan, both of Skidmore, Owings & Merrill, is a product of this rich heritage of balancing aesthetic and functional requirements.

Fazlur Khan, my father, was immersed in the Chicago design imperative from the very beginning of his career. A Fulbright scholarship first brought him to the United States from Bangladesh (then

East Pakistan) in the 1950s. Upon completing two master's degrees and a doctorate in structural engineering he began work at Skidmore, Owings & Merrill (SOM), which had established a reputation of progressive design, quality building, and careful attention to detail. At the time, the Chicago office of SOM was known in particular as a steadfast proponent of Miesian principles of clarity, harmony, and restraint. Shortly after joining SOM, he also became a member of the architecture faculty at the Illinois Institute of Technology (IIT), where he worked extensively with students in the evenings and on weekends. His position at the school allowed him to research experimental ideas he would not otherwise have been able to explore at SOM, and further exposed him to the Miesian architectural philosophy—though Mies was no longer director of IIT's department of architecture, his teachings remained deeply ingrained at the school.

Soon after arriving at SOM, Khan teamed with Bruce Graham (then chief design architect and a general partner), who shared his interest in the honest expression of structure. The two formed an easy partnership, the engineer proposing structural concepts that the architect would craft into architectural space. My father had the rare ability to describe complex engineering ideas in a way that made them both comprehensible and exciting, and Graham's receptiveness nourished his creativity. Their first collaborations were a pair of tall building designs: the thirty-seven-story Brunswick Building and the forty-three-story DeWitt-Chestnut Apartments, both in Chicago. The two projects employed advanced structural systems that led, progressively, to the system they would develop with the John Hancock Center, their next project.[1]

When builder-developer Jerry Wolman approached SOM in late 1964, he had already obtained a site on North Michigan Avenue that bordered a neighborhood of upscale residences and boutiques. Developer Arthur Rubloff had designated this the "Magnificent

Mile" in 1947, in hopes of reviving interest in the area. Nevertheless, corporations and large retailers had remained in the Loop, the city's central business district since mid-nineteenth century. But Wolman, a prescient entrepreneur, was convinced that his site, then used for parking, could support both commercial and residential development. Led by Graham, SOM presented Wolman with two schemes for the 2.8-million-square-feet of building area: a two-tower plan, and a mixed-use, single-tower alternative. The single-tower plan offered a number of advantages: the sole building would cover less of the total site area, leaving more open space for pedestrians; objectionable views between proximate buildings would be avoided; and the apartments would be far removed from the hustle and bustle of the street. In addition, the "world's highest" residences, with their spectacular views of the city and the lake, would command the greatest profit for the developer.

Within the tower, the various uses were stacked by floor: commercial space at the bottom, on a below-grade concourse; five levels of lobby and additional commercial space above that; parking for 750 cars on floors six through twelve; 825,000 square feet of office space on floors thirteen through forty-one; a "skylobby" for the residences at the forty-fourth and forty-fifth floors, including a health club and other amenities; 703 rental apartments (later converted to condominiums) on floors forty-six through ninety-two; and at the very top of the tower, an observation deck, dining facilities, broadcasting facilities, and mechanical equipment. Two television antennae were added, reaching above the 1,127-foot high penthouse roof to the 1,449-foot ceiling set by the Federal Aviation Administration. Cars accessed the parking levels via a concrete spiral ramp structure on the east side of the main tower that connected to it on the sixth floor.

The single-tower scheme was clearly the best programmatic solution, but the cost of construction was an impediment. The architects knew that increasing building height translated to disproportionately higher structural costs per square foot because wind-load effects would necessitate a premium in building material. Traditional types of structural framework were not appropriate for a one hundred-story building; technically they might have been feasible, but they would encumber the developer with an inefficient and economically undesirable building. Faced with this dilemma, Khan determined to introduce a new type of structural system.

In the year preceding the Hancock commission, Khan had worked with a graduate architectural student at IIT, Mikio Sasaki, on a building system that combined diagonal bracing with an exterior column-beam structure to create a highly stable, "trussed tube." Khan and Graham had first used a version of the tubular structural system on the DeWitt-Chestnut Apartments. Based upon this experience, Khan suggested that they implement an advanced and untried version of this new system on the Hancock project. For the thirty-five-year-old engineer, this signified a depth of courage along with a thorough knowledge of his subject. So assuredly did he believe in this structural system that, besides recommending its validity, he predicted that an economic analysis would prove its unparalleled efficiency for a tall building of monumental scale—which it did. Khan proceeded to shepherd the project from schematic design through construction. It was a thrilling few years, and no other project would likewise seize his emotions.

Acceptance of the concept was equally daring on the part of the architect, the design firm, and the developer. Graham remained a steadfast proponent of structural rationalism even as architects began turning away from the International Style and the Miesian principles that they had previously revered. Wolman, too, was swayed by the logic of an efficient and cost-effective structure (the total project cost was a relatively modest $95 million), an unusual and striking aesthet-

Fazlur R. Khan during testing of the floor system for the Hancock Center in April 1965.

ic, and the prestige afforded by a hundred-story tower. A venture-some devotee of construction technology, he was not deterred by lack of precedent. Interestingly, the presumably more conservative insurance firm, the John Hancock Mutual Life Insurance Company, which Wolman brought in to underwrite the development, also concurred with the scale and the pioneering aspects of the design.[2]

The 1,107-foot-tall structure presented a number of challenges to both the engineers and the architects. To accommodate the large floor area needed for the parking levels and offices, and the smaller floor area required for the apartments, the architects introduced a gentle taper. The inward-leaning sides reduce a 47,000 square-foot floor plan at the base to 17,000 square feet at the roof. In addition to serving the building program, this unique shape lowered wind pressures on the tower, and allowed for the composition of an eye-pleasing as well as eye-catching form. The inclined exterior walls, however, raised

5

questions of proportion and floor division. While seeking a compelling building aesthetic and spatial arrangement, the designers had to account for the structural requirements of the trussed-tube system. As a result, office and apartment floor-to-floor heights vary, as do the slopes of the cross-bracing diagonal columns.

Another complication was the aerodynamic response of the building to both sustained high winds and to sudden gusts. Skyscrapers constructed earlier in the century, with their heavy frameworks, were not subject to the degree of horizontal movement that was anticipated for the Hancock Center. That the lightweight, flexible tower would sway far more easily than its predecessors was more of a psychological problem than a structural one—the motion presented no danger to the building's structural integrity. Nevertheless, assurance of stability would do little to calm residents sensitive to motion. But exactly how much movement could a building occupant tolerate before he or she became disturbed? There were no studies on the human perception of building sway at that time, and the design team had neither the schedule nor the budget to commission in-depth psychological research on the subject. Though Khan suspected that occupants of the Hancock Center would not experience objectionable lateral motion, he needed to devise a means to substantiate his belief scientifically.

A solution to this problem presented itself one Sunday afternoon during a family outing to Chicago's Museum of Science and Industry. Walking through the museum, my father holding my hand, we came to a favorite exhibit, Maytag's *The Tale of a Tub*, which featured an enormous (or so it seemed) washing tub elevated on a base for display. The base sat in the middle of the exhibit room on a rotating section of floor, and the clothes drifted in the clear-walled tub. I was fascinated by the slowly swirling clothes, and never tired of returning to admire the phenomenon. This particular Sunday, as we stood on the rotating platform, my father noticed a slight jerk on his hand as he held mine, caused by the floor's motion. The 20-foot-diameter surface, he realized, might serve as a building-motion simulator.

The museum agreed to allow SOM to use the exhibit as a rudimentary testing apparatus. Khan recruited eight volunteer subjects to assist him, and they stood, sat, and lay on the floor in various positions relative to its revolution, and reported their perception of motion and their level of discomfort. From this simple, ingenious procedure, he was able to determine maximum levels of acceptable building motion. And as he had suspected, there was no reason for anxiety about the building's performance in the wind.

The Hancock Center's great innovation is its signature tracery of primary structural members—an exoskeletal truss organization common to bridge design gracefully adapted to a work of architecture. Functionally, this structural system substantially reduced the amount of steel required for the building, saving some $15 million. Moreover, it eliminated the need for internal columns in the marketable floor area.

Referring to the achievement of the Hancock Center, Khan stressed that "a structural solution or a breakthrough is only as good as an equivalent and complementary architecture." For his part, Graham averred that it was in "the gutsy, masculine, industrial tradition of Chicago, where structure is of the essence."[3] In 1969, the two began collaboration on another record-breaking project that would mark the Chicago skyline—the Sears Tower. Completed in 1974, it remained the "world's tallest building" for over twenty years.

The Hancock Center's bold combination of aesthetic and tectonic innovation was received with great enthusiasm. "The parade of diminishing X's," a review in *Architectural Record* concluded, "sets up a dynamic geometry that lends appropriate scale and visual interest to

Following the Hancock Center, Khan and Graham teamed in the design of the Sears Tower (1969–74). Stoller shot this photograph just after it opened, in 1974.

the giant facades." Similarly, attention to detail and appropriate scale on the inside led to the favorable reception of the building's "insulated, tidy, quietly elegant, and tranquil" interior. All the same, some observers considered the giant, aluminum-clad structure to be sterile and dehumanizing. Others found fault with the treatment of the first-story base and the sunken plaza fronting the tower, which they saw as visually and conceptually disrupting. The use of travertine cladding on a steel building also drew some critical attention. The skyscraper's base, one reviewer commented, is "unworthy of the tower above."[4]

Notwithstanding this professional criticism, newspaper reports abounded with excitement and superlatives: deepest caisson, largest joints, highest apartments, fastest elevator. Chicago residents were fascinated by the new high-rise, which they christened "Big John," and were attracted by its bold image. Even before the project's formal announcement, rumors had leaked that SOM was designing a one hundred-story building, and by March 1965 the firm was receiving requests to reserve—years in advance—space in the building.

Construction proceeded rapidly once erection of the superstructure began. Due to a combination of careful detailing and the prefabrication of the immense corner joints, up to three floors were completed every week. In late 1969, as residents moved in, the unimpeded views, acoustic privacy, and convenient location more than compensated for long elevator rides (access to the aparments required transferring from the main elevator bank to local apartment elevators at the skylobby). The *Chicago Sun-Times* effusively reported how one resident, having left a home in the suburbs for the tower, had taken an interest in nature *after* his move to the city. Now, with his expansive view of lake and sky, he could watch the sun rise over the lake, the stars and moon in the sky, and the annual migration of birds.[5]

Architectural photographer Ezra Stoller's interpretation of the John Hancock Center allows one to experience the building's intensity and intrigue. Through crisp lines and bold images, the decisiveness and drama of the external framework unfolds. With corner views, he illuminates the forces of its primary structural components and depicts its massive scale while placing it in the context of its urban environment. He also has managed to communicate a sense of its interior space: the exhilaration of living in a hundred-story tower coupled with the feeling of security derived from its gently slanting walls and garret-like nooks.

The John Hancock Center's clear integration of structural form and architectural space reflects the vital spirit with which Chicagoans—architects, engineers, developers, and residents alike—have embraced the challenges posed by the modern scale of urban tall-building development. Gracefully celebrating the city's crucial role in twentieth-century architecture, the soaring tower remains, thirty-five years after its design, a symbol of innovative and collaborative achievement between architect and engineer.

1. In addition to Graham and Khan, architects and structural engineers guiding the Hancock project were: managing partner William E. Hartmann; administrative partner Albert Lockett; project manager Richard E. Lenke; studio head Robert Diamant; chief structural engineer E. Alfred Picardi; and senior structural engineer Srinivasa (Hal) Iyengar.

2. John Hancock Mutual Life became sole owner of the development in December 1966, when financial pressures forced Jerry Wolman Associates to sell its interest in the project. In 1998, Shorenstein Realty Services purchased the building for $220 million.

3. Fazlur R. Khan, "The John Hancock Center," *The Building Official* (December 1969): 11; Quoted in Dean, "Evaluation," 69.

4. James S. Hornbeck, "Chicago's Multi-Use Giant," *Architectural Record* 141 (January 1967): 141; Andrea O. Dean, "Evaluation: Trussed Tube Towering over Chicago," *AIA Journal* 69 (October 1980): 69; John Winter, "John Hancock Center, Chicago," *Architectural Review* 151 (April 1972): 210.

5. Rob Cuscaden, "'Living in the Sky' is Almost Heaven," *Chicago Sun-Times*, 14 January 1971.

Plates

UPPER AVENUE NATI

Drawings & Plans

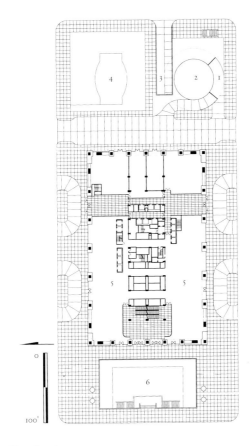

Plan of center

1. RAMP TO GARAGES
2. MECHANICAL
3. SERVICE RAMP
4. CLUB
5. LOBBY
6. COURT

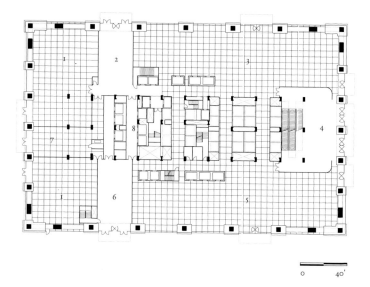

Plan at street level

1. RETAIL
2. RESTAURANT LOBBY
3. BANK

4. OFFICE LOBBY
5. DEPARTMENT STORE
6. APARTMENT LOBBY

7. AUTO LOBBY
8. SERVICE CORE

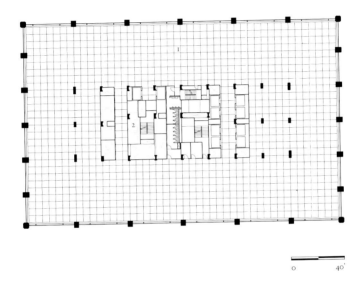

Plan of typical office level, floors 26–33

1. OPEN-PLAN OFFICE   2. SERVICE CORE
   SPACE

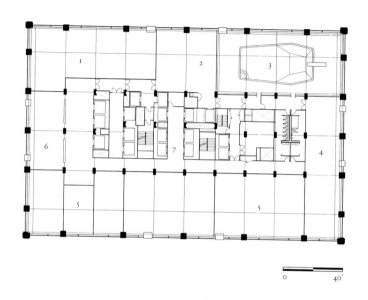

Plan of 44th floor Sky Lobby

1. RESTAURANT
2. RECEIVING

3. POOL
4. HEALTH CLUB
5. SHOPS

6. LOBBY
7. SERVICE CORE

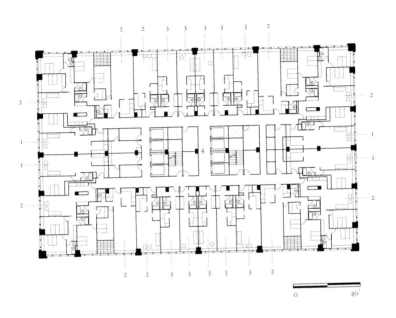

Apartment plan for floors 82–92

1. ONE-BEDROOM
   APARTMENT

2. TWO-BEDROOM
   APARTMENT

3. STUDIO APARTMENT

4. SERVICE CORE

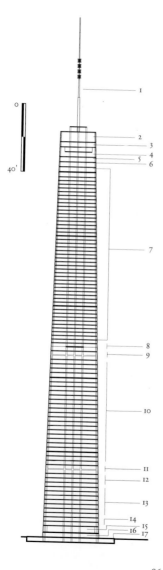

O

40'

Section

Key to Photographs

*Dates refer to the year photograph was taken. All photographs by Ezra Stoller.

Published by
Princeton Architectural Press
37 East Seventh Street
New York, NY 10003

For a catalog of books published by Princeton Architectural Press, call toll free 1.800.722.6657
or visit www.papress.com

Series editor & book design: Mark Lamster
Drawings & plans: Jonah Pregerson

Acknowledgments
I would like to thank my colleagues at Esto Photographics, especially Sara Armstrong, and
at TSI, Mary Milo and Margeris Kimenis, for their help in preparing these images. We are
grateful to Mark Lamster for his support of the Building Blocks series from its inception.
—Erica Stoller

Princeton Architectural Press acknowledges Ann Alter, Amanda Atkins, Nicola Bednarek,
Eugenia Bell, Jan Cigliano, Jane Garvie, Caroline Green, Mia Ihara, Leslie Ann Kent, Clare
Jacobson, Annie Nitschke, Lottchen Shivers, Jennifer Thompson, and Deb Wood.
—Kevin C. Lippert, publisher

For the licensing of Ezra Stoller images, contact Esto Photographics.

Printed and bound in China

Library of Congress Cataloging-in-Publication Data

The John Hancock Center / photographs by Ezra Stoller;
  introduction by Yasmin Sabina Khan. -- 1st ed.
      p.   cm. -- (The building blocks series)
  Includes bibliographical references.
  ISBN 1-56898-259-3 (alk. paper)
  1. John Hancock Center (Chicago, Ill.)--Pictorial works. 2. Joint
occupancy of buildings--Illinois--Chicago--Pictorial works. 3. Chicago
(Ill.)--Buildings, structures, etc.--Pictorial works. I. Title. II.
Series: Building blocks series (New York, N.Y.)
NA6233.C4 J648 2000
720'.483'0977311--dc21   00-009962